Bric-à-brac-adabra

Bric-à-brac-adabra

Poems by

Jean-Mark Sens

Cover design by Shay Culligan
Cover art, *Entitled/Untitled,* by Dominique Sens

ISBN: 978-1-63980-193-0

Kelsay Books
502 South 1040 East, A-119
American Fork, Utah 84003
Kelsaybooks.com

Veritas sequitur esse rei
("truth comes from the being of things")
—Thomas Aquinas

Acknowledgments

Some poems from this collection were previously published in magazines:

Big Muddy: "Object of the Night"

The Comstock Review: "Back Door"

Descant: "Pencil Sharpener," "Potato Peeler," and "Pliers"

I-70 Review: "Light Bulbs"

Malahat Review: "Corkscrew"

Mississippi Valley Voices 20.2 (Fall 2020): "Cotton"

New Orleans Review: "Kitchen Scissors," "Socks,"

nolavie.com: "Cast Iron,"

Poetry South: "Cracked Clay Pot"

William and Mary Review: "Carafe"

Contents

A-C Unit

Trying to buy a breath of winter over summer's heat and humidity
the A-C sweats out mega BTUs to shivers
and all churning in its stomach
guts of freon and windmill inside
blows through its nostrils of a noisy monster
hiccups, stops & goes, neither night or day gives it a break,
and hanging out of the sealed window
it cries down below, despair of higher temperatures to bring down,
not much to reassure, dog days still for long before they bark away.

Alarm

A little red box wired on the wall
a beveled mirror under glass
and a small steel hammer chained below a script line,
silent and ready to auction a call for fire
a countdown of danger
started long ago
a here and now
for an impending call
geared for the in-case, better-prepared, closed-eye scenario
and every day we pass by
at ready like Damocles under his sword.
Someday a man—overall and badge,
comes in, tests it,
a drill foretold,
an exorcism for the real.

Back Door

For Rachel

We came to find a door for the back kitchen whimsical frame.
We did Habitat, Restore City, Second Antiques,
Go Green, Renaissance Project.
After the flood doors came a plenty
salvaged and slid in rows
mute orphans out of their hinges
no way in, no way out
lost to no handle.
Finally, we found the one to the measurements
meshed screens shredded, paint scabbing,
you adopted it
scraped, planed, sanded, brushed it, varnished it
gave its standing allure.
We hung it aligning pins to eyes
with a little feast of dizziness
each holding and pushing till hinges fitted in.
How it swung in coming and going, in and out of its own music
a door restored, like a little miracle,
to let the garden green sieve cool through the screen.

Bed Box

Bed box, dejected,
neighbors dumped out,
standing, its back exposed,
worn spring entrails
love, insomnia,
turn and toss, they squeaked.
No life, defeated and left to poking rain
sound box rhythm lost
last coffin of dreams
laid out and crushed.

Bench

A contemplative of sky and earth
on four with empty slates and a hard back
all open to visions from other eyes
supporting a whole world on its spine,
daily tragedies and comedies,
mothers, fathers sit by the grind of the playground
kids that spin their own merry-go-round,
eye-closed, kissing lovers found and lost in their own mirrors,
a jogger planking down her feet
tightening her sneakers to a dusty imprint,
drunks and dreamers slumbering down,
the newspaper readers full faced of murky and surly dark ink,
and what passes on and by
empty to God's face, fresh green of a wash off from the sky.

Beret

Some poets wear berets,
black felt aureoles—slanted or straight
keeping and building the stream of inspiration
like a lid quivering on a tea pot
dissipating nimbus over the atmosphere
thin Indian smoke signs as they tip off their hats
vapors like dew raising from the fields
a kind of mana, ephemeral, living off the divine
quick and memorable taste
words want to capture, give an image, confide,
aplomb of the exact sound lilting on the tongue.

Books

What I reshelve not books but eyes,
eyes of readers drifting and coming back to call numbers,
all paired and bound under the shutters of bookbinders.
Propinquity and serendipity mingle in the faultlines of sentences
deep gutters of blanks between soundless words and clearing of the
                                                          [mind.
Books and books in lines and rows, an anatomy of mankind
renaming its parts, shelves after shelves
as in an exact chromosomic order.
A lost orphan slid off the family tree,
a monolith ancient classic with a heavy spine, untouched
serving as a semaphore to a linear progeny—epigones and
                                        [commentators,
all scripts asleep deep in the dream of the ink.

I recourse the stacks, officiant of dormant souls,
funerary like what might be left of time in ashes inside urns
soul whiff from the departed,
soft amber shadows like rims around sleepless eyes.

The books return to a grand order, preordained
the common breath of their authors having left the room
a God abandoning the game to its puppets
standing up like guardians of his secrets
tattooed on their backs with marks of their tribes.
They await under the gravity of the dark
to reopen to other eyes, they too will absorb
leaving only incomprehensible tracks, there an insistent bookmark,
dog eared pages, a lingering smell from a surrogate home
all eyes and eyes,
supine, asleep under covers and spines all aligned.

Bottle

Green and empty, lean with a deep punt, inside breast, hilltop. It magnifies years' nourishments: what not to spill, inside world of wine and hope. Eyes see through the thickness of the glass—bright.

Uncorked yesterday, a bottle gurgles into today through the small of its neck—night's purple grapes dripping through stars, breathing out dancing lights. A bottle reveals more than a glass can hold. Unwhispered words lilt on my tongue, woody taste, plush moss, tannins soften to autumn rain, silence slow fallow on my palate— deep wine's riverbed, silt of age sediments marbling red at the bottom.

Empty, a jinni holds in the bottle. Who can see a sun inside one will see two in a second bottle, mind unchecked towards revolving galaxies. So much a bottle holds and can let go, horizon tilted and regained.

Carafe

For Annie-Claude

The carafe stands on the table,
narrow hipped.
Striations combing
round its belly
let water swirl
and cool inside.

A small dew drapes its crystal body,
green, bluish and naked,
giving itself to the slant
light refracts.
A star at the bottom
where the glassblower
twisted it last.

I palm it, pour myself a drink.
It gurgles, trying to hold
its horizon.
I set it back on the rim
it marks,
turn off the lights,
lips wet in the dark.

Cast Iron

We brought a cast iron
deep and grainy
with a lid like a Roman shield
closing over its dark moon face.
It asks for seasoning
the rubbing of oil and fire
dab of garlic and buffing with an oiled cloth
a ritual to the initiation of a growing patina
flame and metal meeting to open its pores.
Solid and indestructible as year after year
heat licked from the outside
building in its own toughening skin
swiped hot cleaned to a new darker copper sheen
piling up memories of stews, terrines, sweating onions,
crimson ebullient tomatoes, thick butternut caramelizing,
nips, Bourguignon, braises and court bouillons
a big anvil of appetite
something to believe in through years of growing
and times in between loving and missing.

Chainsaw

The chainsaw raging against the trunk
insists with stubbornness, and spits gold flakes of sawdust,
straight to the heart of the wood
a wail of human will through the force of shoulders, hands
pushing harder, slicing through rings of ages.
The chainsaw given in to the cutting edge of your insatiable
                                                    [boredom
bartered in your trading despair you call love for the opening of a
                                                    [clearing?
The chainsaw still insists
suddenly roars free—
the tree sawed—giving in, tilts and fells.
A landscape exposing mountain sky in full view
inclines, synclines, slope curves like knuckles of land.
The sun showing now behind blind slats.
you and I, two of the same shades
stripes of a zebra passing the clear of the sky.

Cloche

Fashion French name for a bell-shaped hat
you part your hair under and flap as flappers do.
A grey felt slanted, iris-blue,
a sky of your own that moves around with you,
its own sphere to court birds and a smile,
your own atmosphere transpires under the couvre-chef
sauntering of a catwalk show.

At the party, the glass dome covering pear and cheese
hunger and desire within and without reach
lifting up the cloche like a reality moment of a photography,
joy quick-lived past its revelation.

The cloche hanging from the dresser by the brim
not mean unlike other hats, kind of its kindness,
the mirror glints, shivers of its silver,
deep, receding into a night after the night.

Clock

On the nightstand the alarm clock
a beacon to the silent it punctuates
and continues to take at face value
what it does not repeat
your breathing buried in the pillow
cogs and motions of its hands to the tensed coil of its spring
infinite, binary rhyme within its rhyme
nothing outside the window can interrupt
tomorrow a first day of awakening snow
known even before the alarm rings—
the black ciphers on the white dial
long hand racing the short
a blanched landscape under your eyelids
a road on the top of a hill
thin and sinewy of the first tracks
white glowing fingers
moving companion to an icy moon
soon dripping.

Corkscrew

It is the devil's pigtail
a long curly spiral of metal
a wiggle screw that goes dizzily in the cork
"sacarohlas" they call it in Portuguese
where the tree cork grows
skinned red of its bark for the industry.
All fit, the screw in,
the cork with the waiter's friend
resists philosophically to give in
tightened through old ages
till obfuscate it yields to a pull
popping out in the present its many by-gone years
and delivered from all pressures
bullseye blind on top, red tinged at the lip
disused on the table a mere souvenir
a short breath from a past atmosphere.

Cotton

For Philip

It is what you feel on your skin
wear, worn, underwear
final cause of summer dress, and ironing

long before you even saw the lined up spiny bushes
covering fields and hills swarthy branches
bearing twigs of billions magic moons

bending and swirling to the winds.
Material cause for fibers, carded and hauled to far countries
processed, weaved and rolled to cylinders

plain, printed, mixed, pure, dyed, white, muslin
shirts, robes, chiffons, bandanas, shorts, calico
to the efficient cause of tailors, fashion designers

and left over for paper, stationery makers,
sanitized, balled up, bagged, beauty shops and hospitals.
Of the one and the many, cotton says:

I am only threads from the earth, live short for myself
long in all makings I lend
I live in covering,

I wear in being worn
ragged I return into pages you turn under your hands

in sheets I sleep in company of your body and dreams.

Cracked Clay Pot

with two ear-handles,
round and lipped.
She explained how it cracked
refusing to conform to the strength of her hands
one overlapping the other, then parting, splaying from her palms,
fingers fanning over the wet clay for height and roundness.
Rebellious in the kiln, the pot bubbled, blistered
pigments flared inexplicable colors—
cyan night with a burst of red stars shone in the glaze
and then from the blaze to the coolness of the room
it serrated itself into two perfect twin pieces—
something of a grin curving around the belly, from ear to ear
magic of opening a pot half in half
and closing it complete again
a rent the light comes through
for an instant out of the dark, whole and sole.

Ditch Witch

A ditch and a witch
contraption with chain wheels
a nozzle fitting deep in culverts
underground installations
wire casing, PCV guts
lines of pipes and inner metal tubes.
A mechanical animal shuffling the earth
digs and plies around
to the rambling of its engine
the exhaust of its breathing
its teeth itches digging and tossing
fumes and dust it coughs up through the gravels
all-terrain, dirt it moves and removes.

Double Clippers

The toe clippers
two opposite levers
tête-bêche
cold, and clean Z of inox
a straight beak that closes in a lunule
tight incisives that snap nails into little pieces of their curvatures,
the other side, a sharp, double-sided small sickle
to explore, extract ingrown nails from skin
for beauty excises the impure, even if akin to torture.

8-inch Chef Knife

Tale-tell of the blade
quick nick, nick, nick on the wooden cutting board
by your guiding hand à propos to the cutting edge
glint eye aware to the up and down of your wrist
from whole red bell peppers to little sticks
confetti of collars, ragtime chiffonade
the 8-inch Chef sturdy and forged
Solingen authenticity to never wear
swished, swished swiftly hones on the back of a ramekin
a little grinding music against dullness
here the onion, here the celery, here the split chicken wing
left to right, right to left and again in double steps
quick dance of mincing
omnivorous, devourous as some are amorous
keeping lean against the steel.

Emergency Candles

They slept long with their wicks down
little commas in tallow for pillow
sticks packed by the half-dozen
a blue cat with yellow lit eyes on the wrapper
kept behind the pantry door
the driest place of cool shade
vigils against all weather
bright auras against inclement elements
harbingers of power failures, storm surges, blinding lightning
                                                    [sights.
Single flame, a shimmering eye
into a bottleneck
widening a circle realm of brightness
brought closer to our shoulders flitting the wing sides of the night
a fugitive vision you cusp in the elongated silhouette of your
                                                    [fingers
wind warped to precarious illuminations
lambent swaying steps in the hovering storm
a burning candle holding us close to the aura of its soul wisp.

Face to Face

After François and Jean Robert's photographs *Face to Face*—
"eyes, noses and mouths that tell a never ending stream of silent stories"

Faces objects make to our faces
—door-bolt grimace, squinting slits of a mailbox
the plain gazing wrench of a bold bird,
and the cabinet closing one eye-lock and pulling out its tongue of a
[drawer,
the tight-munching profile of a can-opener,
Made-in-China deep pupils and nose of a three-prong heavy tool-
[sprocket.
Riveted cutter wire beaks return a quick menacing stare
a pocket pair of pliers closed up in profile:
visage objects that glance through our days
unconscious interlopers from manufacturers.

Gar Trophy

The alligator gar, unique of its species,
monster with a long hammer snout
its profile a sardine can opener
greenish, clayous dark with white dorsal flecks
exact, round side eyes of black moon pupils
a pirate submarine from a river oozy mud
with a breathing bladder to gulp the air
a legless alligator with flat prehensile jaws
an amphibious weirdo who like heels bridges rivers through land
hiding breathless in the warm ancestral mud of the bayou for the
                                        [rise of the tide
an armed spindle that weaves the current
and nails holes in its preys
double-row iron teeth
a green bone fish, a rare fellow
breathing in the atmosphere does not kill
species of the living fossils
who dead still finds eternal life
the trophy of it jaws mounted on a fish camp wall still talked
                                        [about.

Garlic Press

For Kristy

Not the cheap one of grey aluminum, the stainless, silver glossy with its ergonomic handles something of an expert, surgical tool, engineered in Germany, cold and solid with its inside fine meshed metal like a pair of nanotechnologically designed tennis rackets closing in. A two-part tool around a pivot doing a somersault almost complete to 350 degrees from its inside to its outside ejecting the pressed clove working smooth to the strength of your fist to bring a sharp effluvium, frills of garlic skin and juice. It is the taboo tool of haute cuisine and meek domesticity—the two extremes classical bringing all to the drop of an essence and country manner taking it whole to the mouth for a ghost-chasing breath—joy in your blood, immunity to bad luck, diseases and vampires.

Hammock

You want a room with a full view
no window and no walls
the sky the only roof over your head

you carry a small parachute of sleep
tri-color—orange, blue, white
shaped like a pod

an eye on each end with a string.
Chaparral, cliffs, oak clearing,
small tundra ash trees

you stretch your hammock
night quietening under your closing lids
the horizon's whispers between your lips

where a road forks
in a cove of trees

suspended
contemplative in nature
a mosquito net for drape
not to be fooled
rest and benevolence rarely mesh in nature.

The hammock sways slightly
till it stills to the deep weight of sleep.

Hot Plate

The coil cold metal
questions what to cook?
Electric element
shape of a maze
red hot
heats pots and pans
no flame
no flambé
does the job
with no passion
no variation, no lick of a blue flame,
said to be safe, provoking no fire
temptation for explosion
desperate asphyxiation
every bottom ghost marked with heat
the coil is coy
a poor mistress can't dance on top of the range
and cold turns back black
dumb, stolid and frigid.

The ink

before you know
echoes in contrast what you think
not to deface a pristine page
engaging sounds and visions
in images beyond ages.
Gone the well to dip in the eye of the quill,
now reduced to powder for laser printers
words retrace readers, writers
marks of their breath and will
smudge, dust, crossed, underlined,
vague or sharp, good or ill
the ink the squid floods what chases to dissipate
and clarifies what the soul finds and anticipates
the ink sympathetic links an inkling
bright into black reveals a sun hidden behind a hill.

Jigger

For Angela

Double-sided tumbler
two cones, against one another,
stainless metal to fill liquor.
It stands on the small end
the jigger's full fill, 1.5 oz, tossed in a glass
and another no matter of the same exact measure
and repeated again, jigger to the drinker
till no one can tell the jigger from the jig.

Kayak

From stern to prow
it stands on the grass
a white stylo against the green
empty manhole nostalgic for the touch of your toes
the agile torso of your strokes
the river sprite splits fast under keel
the paddles course deep
sound running in echoes
perfect palindrome of its name
downstream, upstream
ease and strength
to the rhythm of the flow
now still and empty
thin as a needle
between earth and sky.

Kiln

For Jane

you barely know anything about.
A mysterious apparatus focusing high heat
and dissipating it at a steady baking beat.
Its inner chamber, a miniature temple
the potter inserts three cones like pointed fool caps of clay
testing the bent of the heat.
Offerings of vessels she puts inside—
glow and effluvium of pigments, clay.
A glowing smell in the seizing of a ceramist's work
a Vesuvian miracle pieces will come
intact, glazed or miscalculated
some running lizard tails of cracks
and cool to inescapable basalts, amaranth
cobalt, salt greys, sulfuric yellows, iron reds,
some holding water
some letting sip through forgetfulness.

Kitchen Scissors

For Mark Y

They disassemble to their *grand écart*
orphan of their two blades and reunite to the rivet of their cross
washed they clip greens, make chevrons from folded basil leaves,
opening, closing to the course of your thumb and index
slit the silver belly of a trout in one stroke
cut a parchment paper into a folded heart.
Big chefs disregard them
their feminine emblem of domesticity—
Ariane's friend who cuts a twine to an exact length
tightening a roast to its final cuisson to snap it free.
They split the wings of a chicken
they swoop over the butcher's block like a primitive bird
gaping and closing their sharp beaks—
aerialist of the kitchen, they hang on a nail
sly of two oval eyes.

Knife

When was it last born? Found a hand?
Flint head, honed and honed to a trenchant tool,
felt dangerous, tooth-like, incisive against the skin of the thumb,
became dexterous to cut, whittle, carve and curve,
peel, core, penetrate, bleed, kill and assassinate?
Butt to point—
tipped, edged, heeled, bolstered, rivetted and tangued.
The gymnastic of its cutting,
swift to the rhythm of the wrist.
Knife, its names betray intentions—
dagger, stiletto, scalpel, athame, poniard, bayonet, bistoury, razor
scimitar, box cutter, switch, pen, paring—
knife released from the hand
its silent profile,
a tamed menace inquisitive
exposing what lies beneath the skin.

Light Bulbs

distill the soul of Edison
a same current passing from filament to filament
in volts, watts incrementation on the meter as they fend off the
[night.
Nocturnal in a double life eclipsing into day light
the bulb returns to the thin opacity of its glass house.
One day the switch will turn it off into a final spiff,
a one-flash illumination casting a last purple aura around our
[bodies.
Thrown in the trash
the bulb implodes,
nihilistic, with a suicidal and seductive pop
a glass flower bearing stamina and filaments
precarious and standing
a milkweed bloom of its brilliant hours
void returning to the void of a tenebrous atmosphere.

Magnetic Curtains

The screen over the frame
a thin veil of obscurity
sweeping in the full light of the opened door.
Velcro over the lintel
floating damask closing over in attraction of magnets
twins hugging and parting, reconciling.
Let you see the outside in,
something majestic, the magnetic curtains
palatial threshold magic
splendor of the outdoor to dwell in
an Angel passing,
swift shadow of an invisible visitor
leaving out mosquitoes, flies,
even miasma, summer noise and sultry air.

The Nail

gets it all on the head,
straight, never quivers
a single hand drives in
the line of its body disappearing
blow after blow into the wall.
Its sharp tip entering blind into a beam
fast and deep
it hangs in to be hung on
sleeping in over the years
till a change far from its concerns pulls it by the head
a small squeal bends it out of its ankylosis
a little bit of dust and mortar blows out of its lair
it falls with a single clang on the floor—disused,
a small cyclopic eye of a hole in the wall
patched, covered, blended to oblivion for the new
something to show for all to view.

Object of the Night

The teapot with its blue lid edge
our geography of shoes in the hallway
taking a rest the flaps of their tongues not wanting to break the
                                        [silence
the insomniac neighbor with glass eye in a jar
and the slow paws of the cat, Russian blue, barely brushing the
                                        [headboard
the one-red-dot blinks of the i-Pod
the more than a lifetime of a virtual maze of artists
the door mat, full-face, interrogating the edge of the sky between
                                        [dog and wolf
the crescent eyelash clippers the beautician daughter left on the
                                        [cold marble sink
your mother's ring you place every night over a red hollow
                                        [Daruma head
a little gold circle wedding band certifying nothing but nothing
will move during the length of your sleep and the night
the distance between a pillow and your arm, opened hand,
toward someone there and not there in a story within a story—
                                        [REM abeyance
in absentia of love and lover, the memory path
from your first home you once retraced in the night parterre of a
                                        [Zen garden
out of your feet, out of your mind with hardly a rustle from the
                                        [gravel.

Pencil Sharpener

Baumgarten, double-barrel pencil sharpener. Made in W. Germany

I grind and grind
without complaint.
You hold me tight
between your thumb and index.
You wind me
push in a pencil head,
I unwind long whirls of parasol tops
bite in wood and graphite
every time you push me beyond the break of a line.
This other side of me,
the double barrel, unsatisfied,
longing for some kind of affair:
an artist's fat crayon
the eyeliner of a dancer.
I devour your future words
shaving off your pencil to a sharp head.
You carve unerasable shadows
crisp and incisive
the sharpness of my blade—
dust of your thoughts you blow through me.

Penny

A bit of grime from a flaking cement floor
head scraped from too much shuffling under shiftless shoes
giving a shave to old Abe's face
copper moon tail to scratch a match
across the columns on Lincoln's back.
Blue snap and smell of sulfur
someone lights up under a no-smoking sign.
A lonely penny orphan of a bottom pocket
a warden could not feel through an inseam
—penny fingered and fingered from hand to hand in boredom
for a self-bet, toss of hope or drop
getting out or staying in
penny dropped and rolled
and left again
a puny sun from underground
a centurion's servant in a currency of paupers and pinchers.

Philosophical Stone

Smooth as the inside of your mouth
a hard rock sucked out from the sea
still keeping its mystery
neither dark or day
inside its own galaxy
loose marble from the quarry of creation
a secrecy the pebble holds
cracked would it reveal its true philosophy?
Nothing to hide inside
all matter equals to itself
rift in the grain
outer sheen
inner rougher core
the antithesis of a brick.

Pillow

A silent movie screen
given to closed eyes
dreams light and deep as down feather pillows.

The case smoothed, slapped, turned over, fluffed to new
beginnings
a face imprint, an envelop, unaddressed to an alternate universe
and supine to breathe in
no talk to foretold nights, no screams

nothing to betray
almohado y funda
always in cahoots like shirt tail and pants.

It is the magic lonely people seek,
lie and rely on,
pillow-talk, endless, to no reply.

Plates

Galaxies of white moons around the table
empty mirrors to the fullness of an appetite,
the borderlines of their rims
a portrait of an entrée given to the guests' noses.
How they pass around a revolution
calling to arms knives and forks
their clinks to the hordes of devourers
leaving behind the portraits of their meals
bit and pieces, smeared mustachios of sauces
the yellow sun tail of a yolk.
Plates will return to their blank stares
suds and bright to the eye
stacked to silence
till they shake again to the tectonic motions of the kitchen
                                    [schedule,
the waving goodbyes of waiters' slips dangling over the line.

Pliers

The plight of the pliers is to be held in one hand
in extension of catching and pulling.
Closing/ opening crocodile jaws
pliers come after all acts to twist, snatch, extract.
A wire through a wall, a bend-head, beaten nail
snap, snap, snap, pliers pursue desires for repairs,
a prelapsarian state before any home improvement ever started.
Pliers are cold dreams at the end of a sweat,
the ship surgeon's lie that it won't hurt.
Pliers swing from one hand to another
olive dark metal
inquisitive, reaching further, touching deeper
pull of a string, rebel wire, slanted nut on a bolt,
ambidextrous tool, closing V of near victory,
legerdemain for a triumph: desire and disaster.

Pockets

Inside out, two ears, empty
hanging at the hips
pockets shaped to hands
never wide enough to contain.
One with a little nook for a spare button
a little planet in the darkness of the seam.
They hold all the habits of a day,
in the right side
small serrated beaks of keys,
In the left, with paper butterflies folded inside,
memento, lists, addendum to the day,
a white flag of a kerchief
coughs, tears and rain of all seasons.
Prestidigitator of troves and lost
intimate and coveted,
picked anonymously
a stealth and deft hand through the crowd
exploring for a cellphone and money.
Pockets with their secrets, antics,
insider knowledge of desires
hands always find by the waist
opened and bound,
cul-de-sac,
finger hole of an escape.

Pole Pruners

Sharp beak closing and opening
a one-eye puppet bird of prey
sharp tuff of a saw crest
a pole you dance inside the tree
far above your stealthy hands can reach
slighting branches where fruit hang
at the quick pull of the cord
hit or miss on tiptoe
you clip an avalanche
blushed suns strewing the grass
a dangerous downfall of pomelos.

Potato Peeler

Minimalist, utilitarian wire handle
a thin half-lunar blade
dividing razor-edged slit
a sharp tip to gouge out eyes
thinnest shaver of tubers
extractor of tumors
bruises and calluses
the potato peeler
matter of fact
reveals no truth
beneath the skin
no striptease
peels coil
drowning blop
each victim
touching bottom pot.

Quilt

Feathery angel clouds sewn down between sheets
the quilt companion to the fluffed pillows of sleep
falling silent like flakes over flakes unto deeper snow
the plucked and shaved warmest cover of thousands of fledgings
prized and priced by the weight of their lightness
white of blank dreams like a page
the drop of blood from a quill writes into nightmare.

Razor

sharp
keep quick and short
its blade runs dangerously
erasing the contours of your face
and shows it anew under the lather
smooth like a rebirth
stubble-free in the mirror.
In a ritual,
the razor retraces your symmetrical image
who is you and not you
a last reflection
before turning away for the call of the day.

Reel Push Mower

Sharp and silent
well-oiled as it stands
handle high just at waist level
ready to be pushed
glint of its rotating blade over the lawn
reels roll with a small tic-tac-tic rhythmic of each step
a happy unveiling of a clean turf
linear music birds jump in between
twirls of their notes
the drum spiffing out blades clean
sparrows quick to catch up worms in victory.
Reel to reel, forth and go!
The ritual of parallel counter bands
clearing in to fill out a close crop
turf rolled out to a young green
the mower pursues and ends
to return to the shade of the shed
quivering in its silent
the ray under the door dancing motes
till all die in the dusk.

Rubber Gloves

Ambidextrous—one size fits all
yellow limp hands
hang on the edge of the stone sink.
Tips, knuckles, palms invest them through their flimsy tunnels.
They will adopt anyone, by principles and for action,
up to the sleeve, go for anything our hands can reach—
slick, snappy hands of the murdered, cautious, meticulous,
any print may betray,
the forensic detective's, wanting to remain an omniscient virgin
presence over the scene
a nurse passing cold, ionized surgical instruments under white light
hands soft, blind, blue rubbered to an anonymous touch.
Empty, their little bit of death,
peeled off the intelligence of muscles, bones, flesh
feel-less skin to the touch still reaching for inapprehensible desires
puppets of dumb fingers, defenders from pernicious contagions,
unisex, "made in Mexico" to manikin perfect symmetry
a dumb mirror in their insentient image groping for what the world
                                                    [holds at hand.

Satchel

The satchel retired to the attic
it took dust but didn't lose it Moroccan patina of Saharan sun
and the bellow of its pockets retained its camel smell.
The deep partitions designed for a lawyer, a doctor,
an accountant, nothing I aspired to do and be.
You had gifted to me visiting a souk in Meknes.
The clasps, the strap, not so good, and falling off my shoulder,
cheap copper and the hard hammered rivets to hold the handle.
Almost empty, it dangled down the attic ladder ceiling trap
lowered to a new present, past its exile from our absence—
road of curiosity we had shared, when loving is knowing,
unveiling a mystery
and a map means finding its living shape
the Berbere steep dried paths
goats scattering away through the arnica and gorse underbrush
Notre Dame de l'Afrique far away tiled in red adobe,
its bells ringing among minarets calling for prayer
and the satchel touched the ground, ready to take to the streets
and we both facing each other missing the good of the journey, the
                                                    [destination
like tourists we had contrived to make to a mere souvenir
a displacement of memory old sensations take over—
mere threads of a tire, winds and sands will erase.

Shoes

By two, they go:
gleaming eyes of shined toes
the vaulted arches of feet
soles they bend at every step.
Something like a kiss to a world laid flat
they close a small surface of darkness
and reopen it to the light of each stride.
Shoes take habits wearing on one side
or the other bearing weight, struts of heels
and left on the floor, kicked off
sealing in their inner imprints
like after-image memories or nostalgia
hard feel of cobbles, edges of stairs.
Familiar feet will reenter
repossess them with pulls, pushes, and tightening strings
goading them to new ways
till the one-legged line of a last enjambment
shoes move like a puppet show of our stops and goes.

Shoe Rack and Tree Cloth

The rack in alignment of shoes into by two
little ogling worn out shiny eyes on tops,
straps and stings asking to be pulled tight
soles resting linear miles of memory
muffling dew grass, flip flap cobbles, and crushing cold pebbles
the rack begs questions about the geography of the shoes' journeys.

The tree, hidden under a forest of hats, caps, flung garbs
three footed stands in salute by the door.
The gaping armpit of an old sweater,
limbs divested cloths in limp stillness,
mutual calls and responses to query of gone bodies
their dual questions of a Socratic game
where do we come from, where shall we go?

A few steps away from the threshold,
rack horizontal, tree vertical,
each in place for the coveted silence of peace
stroll and work, unburdened by their owners,
the tree and rack converge
secret conversations when lights turn off.

Shoe String

It snapped in your hand.
Little rat-tail of a shoe string
tightened too many times
from eye to eye
secure to the camber and arching of your sole
retracing its history, hikes, sidewalks, streets, tapping and dancing
six pairs of symmetrical eyes, unblinking, never sleeping,
pull on the tongue
weaved back, ventures ready for adventures,
sure and secure, shoe shod
loose contradicts your footing
tripping in your trips
like a boy who can't knot, and not
prudence to the heart-foolish
tighten your shoes boy.

Soap

Brief companion in the palm of your hand
it blindly retraces your limbs,
escapable, ungraspable, phantom of its smell.
Where was it born, took shape
among candle makers, olive oil traders,
fat to the cameo of its body
thinning and thinning, water slick
rubbed against skin
it cleans, it erases
weariness and sweat,
brightening obscurity
suds as it slows to a last swirl
the drain swallows,
praised for nothing it creates
some say cleanliness is holiness.

Socks

Homozygotes mirroring each other
huddled in a single ball
and separated by the distance of two feet
confounding twins incessantly catching up
ahead and behind one another,
pressures from toe to the bend of the arch.
Stretched, they inhabit their cushioned obscurity
muffling the hardness of the world,
blind folded witnesses spying through the eye of a hole,
the tear of a thread.
At the end of the day
stripped and thrown on the floor
they rest in their own unadorned odor
the fatigue of a day barely seen.
Later they tumble in the water
churned and wrung to an inner silence
till bundled, huddled they reunite in the dresser—
they who do the walk,
worn, yawn off your ankles.

Sprinklers

If you run through the green
at the right time
when the sun pulls down its weight
at the sky's edge
sprinklers fan out multiple rainbows
in a palaver of water.

You can jog through
unbitten by mosquitoes
sweat clears in the twirls
a rain springing from the ground to your head, shoulders and hips
whistling a music,
a rhythm to the speed of your feet
sweeping you at every stride

you disinter the late hour
a lone long-distance runner
cutting through dusk and solid heat
you leap brief escapes from gravity.

Table & Chair

The chair engages the table
no need to be of the same wood,
straight back, flat top,
you nook knees under, cross your feet
lean down your head, crook your elbows.

How the table serves, polished given to the eyes
an everyday altar, gathering of meals
departure of letters, count of coins and bills.
The chair draws and withdraws
bridge of your body to and fro.
The tablecloth you adjust and neat,
sign of a new task,
folded napkin, corporeal, a glass light attracts
a blank sheet, a flag of surrendering,
a space between words incipient of a phrase
a dove tail of white plumes, spirit word.
The hard wood makes table and chair real
paired and different, cut against the grain from the core of a tree.

Cleared, cleaned, wiped the table stands on its feet
to the luminous night the blinds filter through,
the chair secured, parked in full repose of human form
ghost presence gone by morning conferred into sapience
the purring of the fridge, the traffic lights blinking to empty traffic
and once you are awake, whatever your dreams recall
what wouldn't table and chair account of nocturnal witnessing?
Mere objects we assume,
the way given to a new day we miss and dismiss the thankfulness.

Toothbrush

A two-part-word object,
handle and brushy head
so intimate we can't separate
without losing the point of its object.
Rounded and soft bristles
goes up and down, near blind,
a little 32 step dance if fortunate
stopping, gliding, bending
and by the handle, mouth shut
to clean the last specks behind molars.
In and out laid on its back
last light before goodnight
for the next day it stands and understands.

Typewriter

Salvo of letters,
Qwerty keyboard under digits
keys flip across an arc of characters
merely glanced at in kinetic memory
nested levers in a fanned arrangement of springs
words held in suspense, brain and motion,
their sounds catapulted on paper into words
catching up between about to say and already said
page rolls down
return of a hand, sentences under the platen
language made ambidextrous
ring of an end line as catching breath
margin to margin, punch, clutch,
line, and aligned little hiccup of a typo
justified, indented in limits of boundaries
mental turned mechanical
type cast the machine taking imprints of physical habits
part of the wear the forensics can read
smears, broken sets, weak and strong fingers.
Page ending and handed out
a brief white flag of victory
piled up for the next, the typewriter repeats
telling it all, eavesdropped to binary iambics
running and running to no end after a ticking clock on a wall.

The umbrella

opens an injunction against the rain,
double sky of fabric in mourning black,
so taut the drops tease like a tambourine
baleens, rib-folded
better to carry than be sorry.
Carved handle, fake ivory, of a parakeet,
it may dance up and down
the second line choppy band
zoot suits, shiny pumps tapping cobble stones in pirouettes.
If relinquished to its sleepy days
folds its inner darkness,
the wind shows who is the boss
a gust can flop and toss
the umbrella nods to the music
weathered streets that never end.

The vacu-seal

is a simple device, few would deem poetic as meant to fend off wine oxidation. A small piece of rubber like a dreidel, a conic Fez that serves as a surrogate cork, snuggly fitting in the bottle neck with a few pulls on the vacuum pump and clicks of an inner valve. The air sucked out of the bottle leaves a faint smell from another place that went down our throats—deep roots pulling from under reaching for the aquifer, the grape red bled, a covetous hint of a taste the label may describe as wild berries and our tongues try to read under the many rains of by-gone falls, sun seeped down the horizon into the orb of the fruit—maybe a languor and slow fatigue from walking the mile line rows pruning step to step from stock to stock the hirsute ramblings, leaf-tip tongues in flames of Spring—its *vino veritas* early birds already started to unravel with the last chill from behind the mountains, the water raucous running a gulley as passing over open-sky voices into the night earth, the clicks of a sealed-in darkness, a gust sipping under the door, sediments shouldered over the punt.

Votives

Sallow, tallow in bright eye yellow
a candle burns tapering light to the wick
a spirit flame floating shadows incorporeal on the walls
cusp of silence dancing, flickering to the slow giving in
waning darkness and wavering orange tattoos over stones
a one-ogive soul the crypt refracts to its own consciousness
outside plaza St Gregorio with the din of its icon dealers
peddlers of holy paraphernalia, prayer sheets,
herbal remedies, and prophetic scripts
women and men walking under the sun of their century
and here beneath the cobble stones
away from the tremors of traffic and trolleys
a breathed in air of scented holiness under the eyes of St Rita
a plaster saint untouched by the time in mysteries and wonders
for those who can vouch their pity to the world rather than on
                                                    [themselves
desperately hopeful as only irrevocable cases can tell.

WD 40—

a concocted, everyday life miracle against frictions
grime and crank lubricated, water displacement engineering,
wish same way we could swish away ankylosis from our elbows,
mechanics of our bodies, cogs and wheels, in a series of small
                                                    [puffs,
the chain to run smooth at every turn of the pedals
free wheel into an elegant silence of ball bearings
everything released to its own ease for a lighter soul,
moisture behind our sleep-weary lids,
see each other with clarity, eye to eye,
hand in hand before getting up
something simple, an aerosoled genie swipes off everyday's rust
chases out dirt and dust, clear the pipes of our throats to an exact
                                                    [pitch
let words lilt on our tongues, loosened from our unburdened hearts
each moving to one's side of the bed still one touch away
but we fumble all canistered inside
having lost the little red magic wand from the nozzle
unable to remove abrasions, open up the vents of our souls.

Wood Working

he who walks in darkness does not know where he is going for darkness has
blinded his eyes

—1 John 2.11

The spirit level exerts its exactness to adjust the timber,
the point the plane slipped against the grain from the horizon
in a smell of a by-gone forest as you lathed and grooved the planks
the olive wood from the deepening dark of the sun
the sunrise maple of honey auburn wood.
At first, you lifted from rejected pieces simple implements—
spatulas, spoons, letter openers,
small pendants in two or three colors.
A song you must have heard from the veins of the wood
beyond saws, scissors, adze
amplified it between cuts wanting to find praise to the trees
a whistle you carved out of cherry, a flute hollowed from a cypress
something you could play from crowns to roots
a song that opens our eyes to your ears,
lite, light and delight.

X-rays

draw black light out of white bones
reversed image of snow fall caught in a flash.

In and out of sight through a flimsy negative
the orthopedist reads in your neckbone' subterranean map

chthonian sky exploded out of the night
deep shock atoms surface map of hematoma.

She passes her finger over a fault line,
backtracks my clavicle, stops at a radium light storm gap—

dry-ice pain she pinpoints
where you hurt in the picture.

XX Dream Double buugeng

For Lesley

Double X-shaped twin wooden blades
the buugeng player twirls windmills from the strength of his wrists,
folds and unfolds a kinetic of loops and flowing curves
a thin wheeze underlying tune of his motions
unravelling a continuous choreography of circles and ellipses
multiplying rotations of sabers, butterfly wings,
hypnotic dream weaver pursuing the unconscious stream of a river
arrest of a bird, apparitional, brief after-image of its disappearance,
freezing the player divests the buugeng from his ambidextrous
                                        [hands
two X-blades of woods, gleaming wings fallen from an ethereal
                                        [dragonfly
standstill of a fighting game of illusions.

Yoyo

It is the string attached that makes the difference
its pooling a mock perpetual motion
the dizzy dazzling of a color wheel
knotted to a finger
ascent and descent
electric firework that sleeps the closed palm of the player
Yo: claim of the self, a trick of gravity displacement of the ego
Yoyo: ups and downs of the soul losing its bearing
turns and returns of a colloquial kook
Yoyo Ma musing musical, never falling lilt, frontier-less melodies.

Zipper

It displaced the buttons
with the little eye-slits to twist them in and out
close and open.
The zipper with little teeth aligned on a rail
fast up and down, zip and zap,
invented mid-nineteenth century, ending the Romantics,
before it was comprehended in time-efficiency
fastening with no buttons, or strings for boots
not yet overtly admitted expedient for urgency
call of nature, frenzy of love making,
linearity of line like a tram
its car returning to the station
we say up or down setting there an original order
zipper so praised by high fashion designers
and a curse like anything in life once it derails
off-track, teeth splintering apart
a small piece of metal in your hand leaving a gape-hole behind.

About the Author

Born in France, Jean-Mark Sens has lived in the American South for over twenty-five years. He studied for Priesthood at Notre Dame Seminary in New Orleans. He currently lives in South Carolina near Clemson where he works at swu.edu as a librarian.
He published in the U.S. A, England, and Canada.

He has a collection, *Appetite,* with Red Hen Press, and a collection, *Angels & Visitors,* with Wipf & Stock Publishing (2022).

Bric-à-brac-adabra is a collection of short poems that makes manifest the magic of everyday objects in the extra-ordinariness of their ordinary encounters.

www.ingramcontent.com/pod-product-compliance
Lightning Source LLC
Chambersburg PA
CBHW020232090426
42735CB00010B/1659